Young Naturalist's Handbook
INSECT-LO-PEDIA

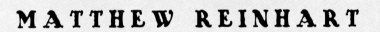

MATTHEW REINHART

HYPERION BOOKS FOR CHILDREN
NEW YORK

This book is dedicated to my family, who always
encouraged my love for insects, although I'm sure
it bugged them a lot.

I would like to thank Dr. Louis Sorkin for his endless
entomological expertise and for correcting all my
mistakes with a red pen.

Type design by Christine Kettner and Eileen Gilshian

First Edition

1 3 5 7 9 10 8 6 4 2

Printed in Singapore

Library of Congress Cataloging-in-Publication Data on file.
ISBN 0-7868-0559-5

Visit www.hyperionchildrensbooks.com

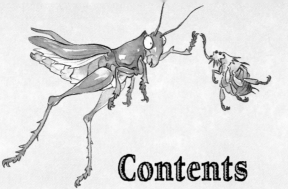

Contents

An Insect Introduction

So what exactly is an insect?

Insects are invertebrates, or animals without a backbone. Instead of having a skeleton inside their bodies like humans, they have an outer shell called an exoskeleton that provides support and protects their delicate organs.

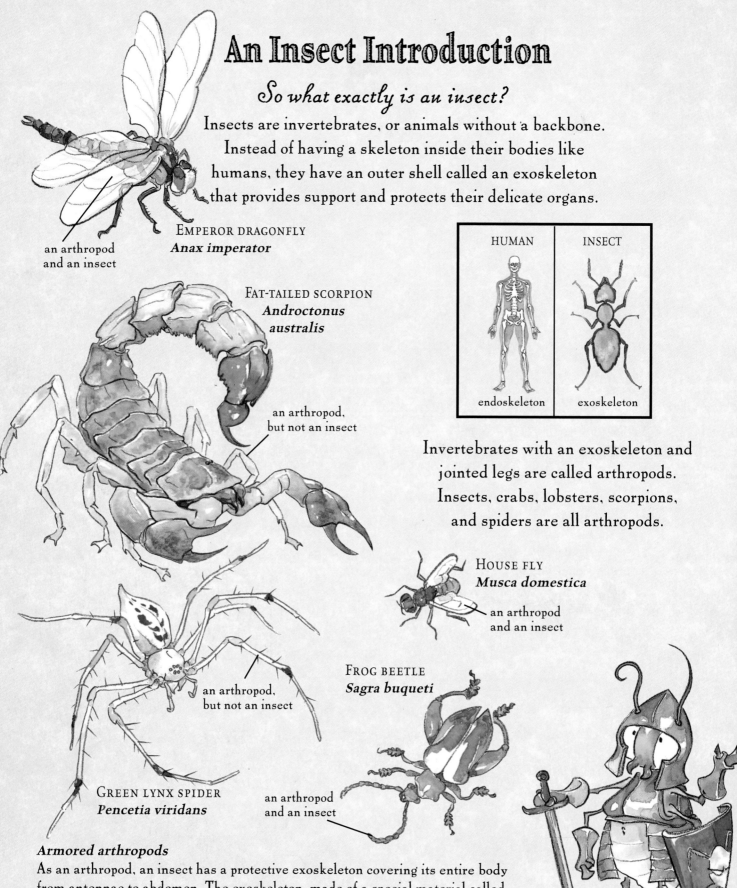

EMPEROR DRAGONFLY
Anax imperator

an arthropod
and an insect

FAT-TAILED SCORPION
***Androctonus
australis***

an arthropod,
but not an insect

HUMAN | INSECT

endoskeleton | exoskeleton

Invertebrates with an exoskeleton and jointed legs are called arthropods. Insects, crabs, lobsters, scorpions, and spiders are all arthropods.

HOUSE FLY
Musca domestica

an arthropod
and an insect

FROG BEETLE
Sagra buqueti

an arthropod,
but not an insect

GREEN LYNX SPIDER
Pencetia viridans

an arthropod
and an insect

Armored arthropods

As an arthropod, an insect has a protective exoskeleton covering its entire body from antennae to abdomen. The exoskeleton, made of a special material called chitin, acts as a suit of armor against natural enemies and water loss.

4

SALLY LIGHTFOOT CRAB
Graspus graspus

an arthropod,
but not an insect

GIANT CENTIPEDE
Scolopendra gigantea

an arthropod,
but not an insect

Molt-mania
An insect must shed its skin, or
molt, as it becomes bigger and grows a
new, larger exoskeleton. Insects like the
mayfly molt as many as fifty times
in their life! *And you thought* you
went through a lot of clothes!

Elephant-sized Ants
Humankind shouldn't ever have to worry about an attack from giant
mutant ants. A chitin exoskeleton is perfect for small animals, but it
isn't strong enough to support one weighing more than a quarter of
a pound. A molting mutant ant the size of an elephant would be
crushed under its own weight before its
new exoskeleton could harden. *What a relief!*

Unlike other arthropods, an insect body is divided into three distinct
segments (head, thorax, and abdomen) and includes three pairs of legs.
The word *insect* comes from the Latin word meaning "to cut into,"
referring to these body segments.

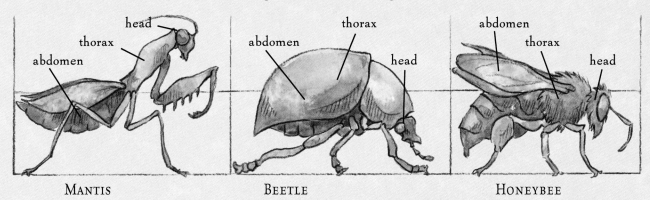

MANTIS — head, thorax, abdomen

BEETLE — abdomen, thorax, head

HONEYBEE — abdomen, thorax, head

5

A Peek Inside: Insect Anatomy

The Head: Center for the Senses

Much of an insect's important equipment for taking in
sensory information is located on its head.

Eye see you!
Most insects see with the help of compound eyes. Made up of thousands of tiny lenses,
compound eyes are very sensitive to movement, light changes, and many different colors.
The compound eyes of bees and butterflies can even see colors invisible to human eyes!

Munchin' mouthparts
Insects have different mouthparts adapted
for eating specific kinds of food. Beetles,
grasshoppers, and ants have jaws called
mandibles to slice, chop, and chew food.
Mosquitoes stab into skin and suck
up blood with needlelike mouthparts.
Butterflies and bugs have hollow
tongues for slurping up liquid food.

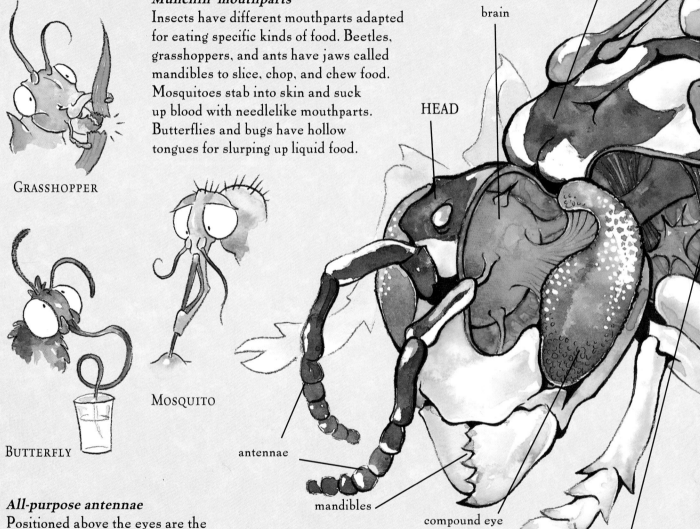

GRASSHOPPER

MOSQUITO

BUTTERFLY

THORAX

brain

HEAD

antennae

mandibles

compound eye

flight muscles

All-purpose antennae
Positioned above the eyes are the
sensitive antennae. These flexible
feelers are used for touch, sound,
smell, and taste.

The Thorax: Middle with Moving Parts

Three pairs of jointed legs for walking, swimming, or climbing attach to
the thorax, or the midsection of an insect. Insects are unique among
invertebrates in that they are the only ones to have evolved wings!

6

heart

gut

ganglia

ABDOMEN

spiracles

Flexing for flight
The muscles inside the flexible thorax enable the wings to flap. Butterflies can only flap their large wings four to twelve times per second, but the wings on buzzing mosquitoes move up to 600 times per second! *I get tired just thinking about it!*

Miracle spiracles!
Insects don't have lungs, but they do breathe through tiny holes in their abdomens called spiracles.

hind leg

Blood bath
Without veins to carry it around like human blood, insect blood swishes over muscles and internal organs with the help of a simple heart.

forewing

tarsus (foot)

Brain chain
An insect brain processes information from the eyes, antennae, and mouth. A chain of smaller brains called ganglia controls different sections of the body. If part of an insect is hurt, the rest of its body continues to function. A cockroach can live a week without a head, but eventually dries up because of the break in its exoskeleton.

The Abdomen: Everything Else
The flexible, segmented abdomen of an insect contains all the insect's machinery for digestion and reproduction. Most of the gut and sexual organs are located in the abdomen.

Life Cycle

Throughout an insect's life, its body goes through a series of changes, or a metamorphosis.

egg   nymph   nymph   adult

You look just like your mother. . . .
Some insects undergo an incomplete metamorphosis, beginning life as a wingless nymph that looks similar to an adult. After emerging from an egg, a grasshopper nymph looks much like a smaller, wingless copy of its parents. With each growth spurt, the nymph sheds its skin, and gradually takes on an adult form.

Were you adopted?
A complete metamorphosis begins with the young insect, or larva. The larva has a completely different shape than its parents. The skin of a wormy larva molts as the larva grows larger, which soon leads to a second form called the pupa. After it takes some time to rearrange its body, the pupa then splits open as the adult emerges. Caterpillars undergo the most famous metamorphosis into winged moths and butterflies.

egg   larva   pupa   adult

Communication

Like people, insects have many ways to communicate with one another.

Sound
The male cricket chirps a mating song by rubbing together bumps on its front wings.
Keep it down, Romeo!

Color and Pattern
Like a flashing caution sign, the poisonous monarch butterfly displays bright warning colors to any predators foolish enough to attack.
Warning: Don't eat me.

Touch
A stroke from an ant's antenna on the cheek of another ant can be a sign of danger or a request for food.
Touchy-feely.

Actiou

The wiggly, shaky dance of a honeybee shows other bees in the hive where to find new flowers. *Boogie down, bees.*

Smell

Moths and butterflies release chemical messages called pheromones into the air that other moths can smell and understand. *Smells like love in the air!*

Defense

Insects need more than just a hard exoskeleton to stay safe from hungry enemies.

◄ **Thorny threats**
An exoskeleton covered with prickly spikes and needles is one way insects fight back against attackers. A swift kick from the spiked legs of a New Guinea stick insect sends predators packing!

Deadly dinner ▶
Making a meal of the colorful but poisonous pygomorph grasshopper of Africa can be a fatal mistake for hungry birds, mammals, and even humans!

◄ **Have you seen Larry?**
Many insects camouflage or disguise themselves to fit in with their surroundings. Looking like a dried leaf, the Indian leaf butterfly is completely invisible to its enemies as it hangs from tree branches.

Trick or Treat ▶
Insects also copy or mimic the appearance of dangerous animals or inedible objects. To keep from being eaten, the caterpillar of the swallowtail butterfly disguises itself as a slimy pile of bird poop. *Eew!*

Feet, don't fail me now! ▶
Many insects are just too fast to catch. When discovered, a domestic cockroach scurries to safety with long, slender legs made for running. Wings are another important way to escape danger. The powerful wings of expert aviators like houseflies react to even the slightest movements and allow them to jet away from oncoming flyswatters. *Ha-ha—you missed me!*

9

The Origin of Insects

Millions of years before dinosaurs ruled the earth, prehistoric insects colonized the land and took to the skies. The earliest known fossils of primitive insects are 300–500 million years old! Prehistoric insects like giant dragonflies and cockroaches began to appear soon afterward. Scientists who study the fossil remains of ancient insects, called paleoentomologists, believe insects evolved from long multilegged creatures.

A sticky situation
Prehistoric insects were lured to the sweet scent of tree sap and often trapped in the sticky goo. Over time, the sticky sap hardened into a transparent jewel-like substance called amber that preserved the insects' bodies perfectly.

INSECT FOSSIL
Ancient dragonfly preserved in hardened rock

Prehistoric helicopters
Prehistoric insects were some of the largest ever recorded. Fossils of the prehistoric dragonfly *Meganeura mongi* have a 2½-foot wingspan!

10

Living in the past
The velvet worm may be a distant ancestor of today's insects. Looking like a bizarre science experiment, this "walking worm" has a long soft body with clawed legs and pointy mandibles.

Glide ride
The first winged insects probably did not flap their wings to actually fly. Instead, they might have used them to glide with the breeze.

VELVET WORM
Peripatoides novozelandiae

The appearance of flowering plants in the Cretaceous period about 100 million years ago caused an explosion in insect evolution. Flowers presented a new source of food—nectar—to the early ancestors of present-day bees and butterflies. So as *Tyrannosaurus rex* stomped through prehistoric forests, new types of insects buzzed around it, in search of a sweet nectar treat.

Distribution

More than a million different kinds of insects inhabit the world in a huge variety of shapes and sizes. Insects are incredibly adaptable creatures. Due to their small size, protective exoskeleton, wings, and fast reproductive cycle, they have found a home in just about every habitat in the world. That makes them the most successful animals on earth!

Insects occupy every land mass on the planet, north to south, including the Arctic and Antarctica.
Maybe that's why they call it ANTarctica!

Insects aren't just a bunch of land lovers. Aquatic insects such as diving beetles and saucer bugs populate freshwater lakes, rivers, and puddles.
Marine insects live on the surface of salt water and ride the waves. ***Surf's up!***

11

Bristletails

long antennae

humped back

One of the most primitive insects, the bristletail gets its name from the whiskers on the underside of its abdomen. These bristles, called styles, help these humpbacked little insects hold on to steep rocks and terrain.

Who needs hiking boots?

eyes placed on top of head

Safety in a snap!
A jittery bristletail escapes danger by flicking the ground with its hairy tails and jumping away.

SEA BRISTLETAIL
Petrobius maritimus

8.1 7.9 10.0

3 tails

It's all Greek to me!
The scientific name for a bristletail is *Archaeognatha*, which means "ancient jaw" in Greek, for its primitive mandibles.

COMMON SILVERFISH
Lepisma saccarina

Silverfish and Firebrats

scale-like body segments

Nearly blind, the silverfish is a scaly, wingless insect with a teardrop body ending in three long tails. Like a vampire, this simple insect is nocturnal, or active in the darkness, and hides to avoid bright light. Colored with metallic patches of silver, a fleeing silverfish resembles a swimming fish as it wriggles across the ground.

tiny eyes

three tails

Mmm—delicious!
Silverfish are household pests that enjoy a diet of fabric, books, and wallpaper paste.

Brats in the bakery
As a lover of starches and sugary foods, the firebrat, a heat-loving cousin of the silverfish, often makes its home in bakeries.

Mama loves me!
Some silverfish care for their young in small tunnels underground.

It's all Greek to me!
The scientific name for silverfish and their relatives is *Thysanura*, which is Greek for "fringe tail," for their three pointed and fringed tails.

ADULT EUROPEAN MAYFLY
Cloeon dipterum

Mayflies

More than 300 million years ago, the ancient ancestors of the mayfly were probably the first insects to grow wings. Most present-day mayflies are fragile flying insects with two pairs of clear, triangular wings. Breathing with special gills, mayfly nymphs can live underwater for years. Adults, however, only live for a day or two.

two pairs of veined wings

strong legs for gripping rocks and plants

abdominal gills for aquatic life

MAYFLY NYMPH

Insect teenagers
Mayflies are the only insects with a winged adolescent stage, called a subimago. The subimago flies a short distance, then molts its skin to become an adult.

wings fold together over back

It's all Greek to me!
The scientific name for mayflies, *Ephemeroptera*, which means "short-lived wing" in Greek, is appropriate, since adult mayflies have a life span of only a few days.

PRONGILL MAYFLY
Leptophlebia vespertina

Dragonflies and Damselflies

Dragonflies and damselflies are hovering, high-speed hunters. A dragonfly really lives up to its name with its large colorful body, powerful wings, and biting mandibles. Its delicate cousin, the damselfly, is a weaker flier with a long, skinny abdomen. Unlike its parents, the nymph of a dragonfly or damselfly is adapted for underwater life in ponds or lakes.

EMPEROR DRAGONFLY
Anax imperator

AZURE DAMSELFLY
Coenagrion puella

wings fold over its back, like all other damselflies

BROAD-BODIED CHASER DRAGONFLY
Libellula depressa

It's all Greek to me!
The scientific name for dragonflies and damselflies is *Odonata*, which means "tooth" in Greek, for their powerful jaws.

Even an aquatic dragonfly nymph is a lethal predator. The nymph's head has a special hooked mask used like an extra arm for snatching unsuspecting prey, such as fish and tadpoles.
Watch out for this kid!

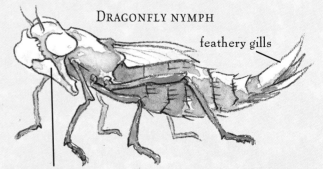

DRAGONFLY NYMPH

feathery gills

clawed mask for catching underwater prey

1. Lunch swims by....

2. Gotcha!

Turbo-tush!
When in danger, a dragonfly nymph can make a quick escape by shooting a jet of water from its rear end!

14

GIANT HELICOPTER DAMSELFLY
Megaloprepus coerulatus

long, thin abdomen

A distressing damsel
The wingspan of the giant helicopter damselfly, the biggest of all damselflies and dragonflies, measures up to six inches across, and its tail sometimes measures as much as 5½ inches long!

BEAUTIFUL DEMOISELLE DAMSELFLY
Calopteryx virgo

shiny, metallic exoskeleton

CLUB-TAILED DRAGONLFLY
Gomphus vulgatissimus

Don't forget your sunblock!
A dragonfly warms up for flight by shivering its wing muscles or basking in the sunlight.

Speed Limit
30 MPH

Speed freaks
The Australian dragonfly *Austrophlebia costalis* has been clocked at speeds of thirty-six miles per hour!

She's got eyes in the back of her head
Dragonflies have excellent vision in nearly all directions. The compound eyes of a dragonfly contains about 30,000 lenses and take up most of its head.

I'll have that to go!
Dragonflies don't stop to eat their meals but remain in flight as they dine. A single dragonfly consumes thousands of mosquitoes, flies, and other insects in its short lifetime.

15

STRIPED EARWIG
Labidura riparia

Earwigs

pincers, or cerci

The long, flattened body of an earwig is made for squeezing into tight spots. Earwigs don't really crawl into people's ears to bite their eardrums, as myth would have it. Instead, these nocturnal scavengers live under rocks, bark, and leaves. The most distinctive features of an earwig are its short, hardened wings and the two defensive pincers on its rear end.

COMMON EARWIG
Forficula auricularia

GIANT AUSTRALIAN
EARWIG
Titanulabis colossea

See you later, Mama!
A mother earwig cares for her 20 to 50 eggs and protects her newborn in an underground burrow. Unfortunately, her motherly behavior doesn't last too long. Soon she encourages her children to leave by attacking and eating them!

Batty, ratty earwigs
One kind of earwig lives in the fur of Asian bats, another in the fur of African rats. Hairy and nearly blind, these tiny earwigs crawl through a host's fur feeding on dead skin. **Yummy!**

It's all Greek to me!
The scientific name for earwigs and their relatives is *Dermaptera*, which in Greek means "skin wing."

Cockroaches

AMERICAN COCKROACH
Periplaneta americana

protective thorax, or pronotum

Cockroaches are the true survivors of the insect world. Fossilized remains of their ancestors are more than 300 million years old! An ideal scavenger, the cockroach eats just about any dead plant or animal matter it comes across. When danger approaches, it quickly scuttles or flies away and squeezes its flat, leathery body into a narrow space. Used as feelers in the dark, its sensitive, threadlike antennae alert it to the slightest vibrations.

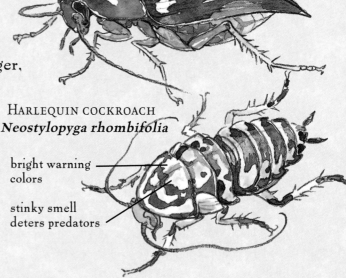

HARLEQUIN COCKROACH
Neostylopyga rhombifolia

bright warning colors

stinky smell deters predators

16

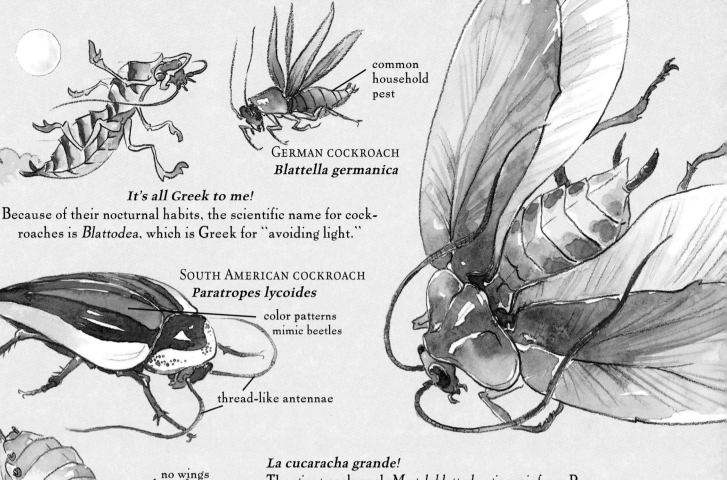

common household pest

GERMAN COCKROACH
Blattella germanica

It's all Greek to me!
Because of their nocturnal habits, the scientific name for cockroaches is *Blattodea*, which is Greek for "avoiding light."

SOUTH AMERICAN COCKROACH
Paratropes lycoides

color patterns mimic beetles

thread-like antennae

no wings

spiracle

La cucaracha grande!
The giant cockroach *Megaloblatta longipennis* from Peru and Ecuador can grow up to eight inches long and has a wingspan of one foot!

Having a hissy fit
When startled by larger animals, the Madagascan hissing cockroach raises its rear end in the air and forces air out of its tiny breathing spiracles, hissing like a snake!

Of the 4,000 kinds of cockroaches on Earth today, only about one percent are household pests. These insect invaders adapted quickly to human homes, feeding on food scraps, leather, soap, wood, and even plastic. Despite deadly insecticides and the occasional heavy shoe, the domestic cockroach continues to flourish, reproducing in large numbers and spreading disease.

Babies on board
The female cockroach only mates once, but stays pregnant for the rest of her life! A mother cockroach carries an egg case filled with 12 to 40 eggs at the end of her abdomen until she finds a suitable place to leave it.

Baby on Board!

17

Termites

Masterful insect architects, termites build elaborate and sometimes massive underground nests as community homes. As a highly social insect, each termite fills a specific role within the colony.

At the center of the colony, the termite queen is the egg-laying machine for her nest, producing thousands of eggs a day from her bloated abdomen. The king termite waits near his queen to fertilize her eggs. Blind male and female workers gather food, care for the royal pair, and maintain the nest. Menacing soldier termites with armored heads and dangerous mandibles defend the colony from any threat.

AFRICAN TERMITE
Macrotermes suhyalinus

huge, throbbing abdomen as big as a human thumb

male or female

shed or bitten-off wings

WINGED REPRODUCTIVE TERMITE

TERMITE KING

special chemical-making gland inside head

sharp mandibles

blind

surprised ant

TERMITE SOLDIER

TERMITE WORKER

Soldiers, prepare to fire!
Soldier termites don't just use mandibles to protect their colony. The fatheaded soldiers of snouted harvester termites have pointy snouts that squirt chemical goo at unwary attackers.

Old insects
King and queen termites have a life span of 20 to 50 years!

18

Termite tower

Rising 40 feet above the ground, the massive colony mounds of the West African termite act as natural air conditioners. Warm air vents from the top of these hollow chimneys cool the entire nest on hot days. They are also perfect scratching posts for passing elephants.

heat chimneys

hot air rises out

It's all Greek to me!

The scientific name for termites is *Isoptera*, meaning "equal wings" in Greek, for the equal-sized wings of queen and king termites.

workers tend fungus crop

queen inside royal cell

There's a fungus among us

Several termites from the savannas of Africa and Asia grow fungus farms within their nest. The fungus feeds on termite waste and the termites in turn eat the fungus for food. *Waste not, want not!*

eggs in larva gallery

nest's exit/entrance tunnel

Stoneflies

Stoneflies are weak fliers whose transparent wings fold over their flat, double-tailed abdomens. Though few insects can survive cool climates, stoneflies thrive in the cold and, as with the small winter stonefly of North America, even mate in the winter!

YELLOW SALLY STONEFLY
Isoperla grammatica

COASTAL STONEFLY
Neoperla clymene

Two taps mean "I love you"

During mating, a male stonefly taps his abdomen against the ground to attract a mate. Soon a female will tap a response of her own to his rattling, stonefly love song.

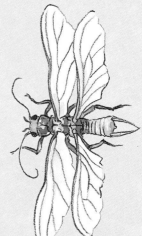

It's all Greek to me!

The scientific name for stoneflies is *Plecoptera*, which in Greek means "wicker wing," for the interwoven veins on their wings.

Grasshoppers and Crickets

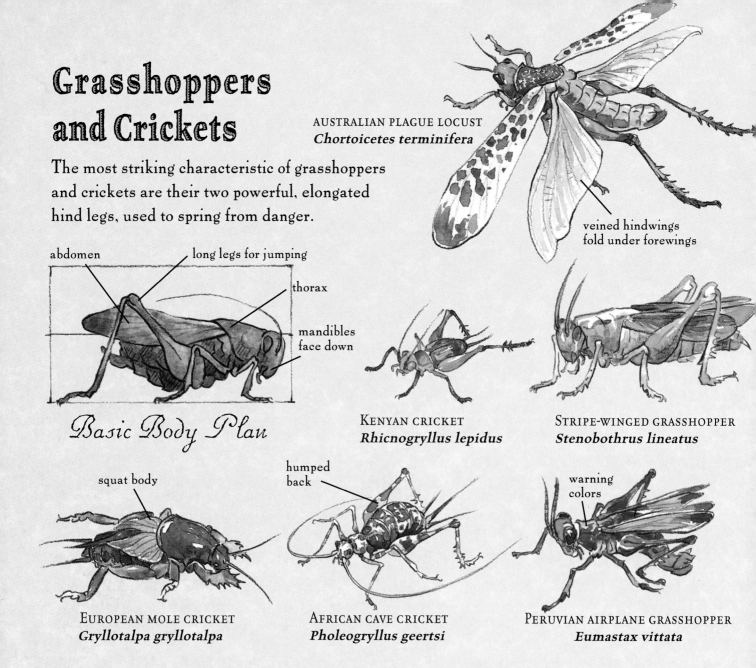

AUSTRALIAN PLAGUE LOCUST
Chortoicetes terminifera

veined hindwings fold under forewings

The most striking characteristic of grasshoppers and crickets are their two powerful, elongated hind legs, used to spring from danger.

abdomen

long legs for jumping

thorax

mandibles face down

Basic Body Plan

KENYAN CRICKET
Rhicnogryllus lepidus

STRIPE-WINGED GRASSHOPPER
Stenobothrus lineatus

squat body

humped back

warning colors

EUROPEAN MOLE CRICKET
Gryllotalpa gryllotalpa

AFRICAN CAVE CRICKET
Pholeogryllus geertsi

PERUVIAN AIRPLANE GRASSHOPPER
Eumastax vittata

Grasshoppers and crickets are varied in shape and habitat. Mole crickets are squat, underground miners with broad, shovel-like forelegs. In darkened caves, near-blind camel crickets use their extremely long antennae to sense danger or feel for food. Bizarre, leaflike monkey-hoppers camouflage themselves as the plants of their tropical homes.

What did Katy do, anyway?
Perfectly hidden among plants, the katydid often mimics leaves or bark. This vocal cousin of the grasshopper has a mating song that sounds as if they are chirping, "Katy did!"

Ah, the sound of love!
Grasshoppers and crickets are talented noisemakers that sing by rubbing their forewings or ridged legs together. Ears on their abdomens or front legs allow them to hear these songs and find a new mate.

Colossal crickets
Found only in New Zealand, the nearly extinct wetapunga is a massive plant-eating cricket that measures 3½ inches long and weighs nearly 3 ounces (that's a lot for an insect).

leg spines

displays warning colors if attacked

WETAPUNGA
Deinacrida heteracantha

KENYAN KATYDID
Dioncomena ornata

Cricket thermometer
The tree cricket is a natural thermometer. By counting the number of chirps it makes in an hour and adding 40, we can find out the temperature in Fahrenheit degrees.

It's all Greek to me!
The scientific name for grasshoppers, crickets, and katydids is *Orthoptera*, which means "straight wings" in Greek, for their tough, straightened forewings.

Home, Sweet Home

Flash, splash, and dash!
Many grasshoppers hide a pair of bright-colored wings under their camouflaged forewings. If danger gets too close, the African bush hopper leaps away, flashing its bright red wings and squirting a foul, foamy chemical that distracts the pursuing predator.

Home Sweet Leaf
A leaf-rolling cricket builds a nest with curled leaves.

Warts be gone!
Up until the turn of the twentieth century, warts were cured with the help of a wart-biter cricket. After biting the wart off, the aggressive little cricket vomited a digestive liquid over the wound which was thought to keep more warts from growing back.

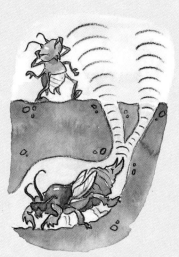

Pump up the volume!
Humans weren't the first animals to invent the speaker system. Mole crickets dig elaborate underground tunnels that act like stereo speakers for amplifying their mating calls.

21

Stick and Leaf Insects

Stick and leaf insects are camouflaged phantoms that move slowly and unseen through their tropical homes. With its slender, knobby body, the stick insect or walking stick mimics the very branches on which it lives. Looking like a pile of leaves, the leaf insect has a wide, flattened abdomen and jagged leaf-shaped legs.

It's all Greek to me!

The scientific name for walking sticks and leaf insects, *Phasmatodea*, meaning "ghost" in Greek, is appropriate since the bugs are nearly invisible in their leafy environment.

up to four inches long

broad, leafy legs

small antennae

leaf-shaped abdomen

ASIAN LEAF INSECT
Phyllium siccifolium

Insects incognito

A leaf insect wears several disguises through its lifetime. The egg of a leaf insect often resembles a seed or pebble. After birth, a young leaf insect looks like a nasty red ant. Only as an adult does this insect pretender take on a leafy appearance.

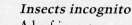

True colors

A leaf insect can adjust its skin color, depending on the time of day. During daylight hours, its exoskeleton appears paler in color, while at night it shifts to a darker tone.

A big stick

Walking sticks are among the longest and largest insects in the world. One tropical species, *Phobaeticus serratipes*, measures 13 inches long!

If attacked, the striped *Anisomorpha buprestoides* throws up, or regurgitates, its last meal at predators. The Florida stick insect protects itself from predators by squirting a foul-smelling chemical so powerful it can knock out a human being!

spined thorax

thorny, branch-like legs

MACLEAY'S SPECTRE
Extatosoma tiaratum

mandibles of a plant-eater

female disperses eggs by flicking her tail

NORTHERN
ROCK CRAWLER
Grylloblatta campodeiformis

Rock Crawlers

Rock crawlers are hunched, wingless insects that inhabit cool northern forests, mountains, and caves. Rock crawlers, often called ice bugs, cannot survive in warm climates and are typically found scurrying over ice and snow. *I hope they stay out of my ice cream!*

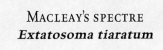

It's all Greek to me!

Since rock crawlers look like a cross between a cockroach and a cricket, their scientific name is *Grylloblattodea*, which means "cricket roach" in Greek.

Mantids

Commonly called a praying mantis, the mantid is a ghoulish insect predator that grabs its unsuspecting prey with large hooked forelegs. At rest, its powerful forelegs fold beneath a triangular head and elongated thorax as if in prayer. Stealthy hunters, mantids may camouflage themselves as leaves or flowers and remain completely still before pouncing on prey.

Fatal foliage
With color that matches its flowery home, the Maylasian flower mantis waits for its next victim disguised as an orchid and nearly invisible to the eye.

It's all Greek to me! The scientific name for mantids is *Mantodea*, which means "like a prophet."

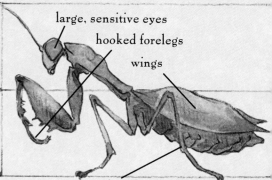

large, sensitive eyes
hooked forelegs
wings
long hindlegs

Basic Body Plan

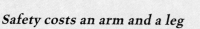
camouflaged body color

PRAYING MANTIS
Mantis religiosa

Safety costs an arm and a leg
Mantids will sacrifice a walking leg to a predator in order to escape. By contracting a muscle at the base of the limb, the mantis releases the leg and, if the insect is young enough, grows a new one.

Take that, you bully!
Mantids have other defenses besides camouflage against enemies like birds and lizards. Less aggressive mantids can quickly run or fly away, while braver ones stand their ground and try to appear larger by spreading out their colored wings and forelegs. When an attacker gets too close, a desperate mantis will strike out with its spiny forelegs to inflict a painful pinch.

24

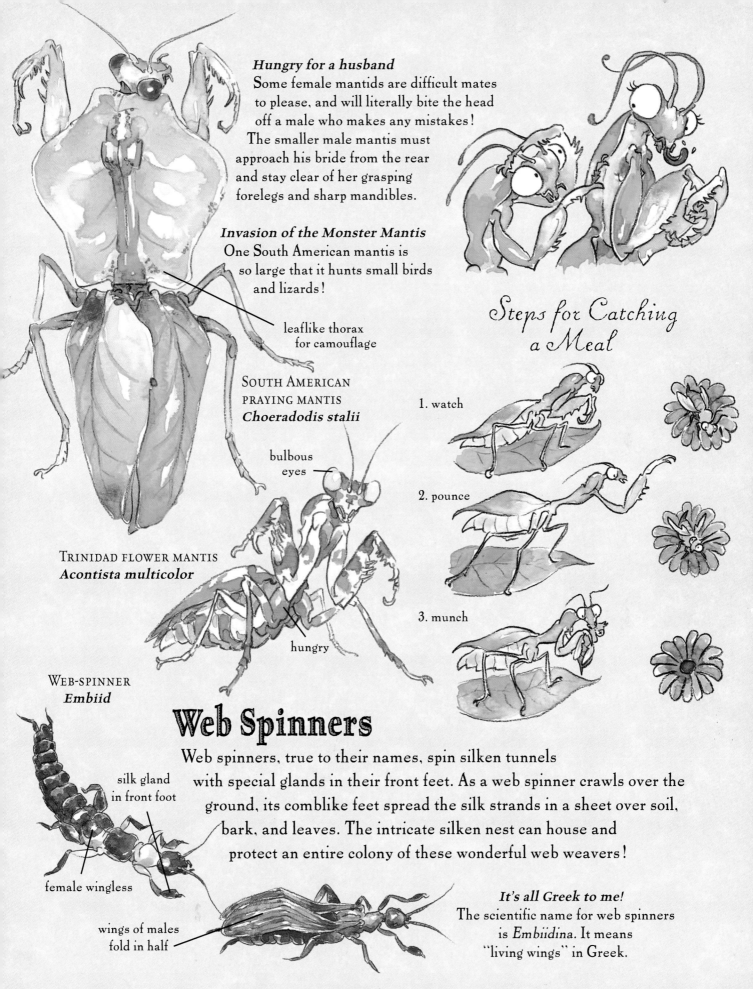

Hungry for a husband
Some female mantids are difficult mates to please, and will literally bite the head off a male who makes any mistakes! The smaller male mantis must approach his bride from the rear and stay clear of her grasping forelegs and sharp mandibles.

Invasion of the Monster Mantis
One South American mantis is so large that it hunts small birds and lizards!

leaflike thorax
for camouflage

SOUTH AMERICAN
PRAYING MANTIS
Choeradodis stalii

bulbous
eyes

TRINIDAD FLOWER MANTIS
Acontista multicolor

hungry

Steps for Catching a Meal

1. watch

2. pounce

3. munch

WEB-SPINNER
Embiid

silk gland
in front foot

female wingless

wings of males
fold in half

Web Spinners

Web spinners, true to their names, spin silken tunnels with special glands in their front feet. As a web spinner crawls over the ground, its comblike feet spread the silk strands in a sheet over soil, bark, and leaves. The intricate silken nest can house and protect an entire colony of these wonderful web weavers!

It's all Greek to me!
The scientific name for web spinners is *Embiidina*. It means "living wings" in Greek.

25

Book Lice and Bark Lice

Keep this book away from hungry book lice! These scavenging insects with scraping mandibles enjoy a diet of flour, books, and other paper products. Book lice are known to squeeze their flat soft bodies under wallpaper and between furniture cushions to make a home.

It's all Greek to me!
The scientific name for book lice and their relatives is *Psocoptera*, which means "grinding wing" in Greek.

splotched wings

BOOK LOUSE
Liposcelis terricolis

BARK LOUSE
Pscococerastis gibbosa

Country cousins
Their outdoor relatives, called bark lice, inhabit cracks in tree bark and feed on pollen and fungus. Winged bark lice are social and often move around in groups.

Parasitic Lice

Lice are parasites, or creatures that live and feed on or inside a host animal. Parasitic lice choose a number of different hosts, including elephants, guinea pigs, and apes. Crawling through skin and hair with hooked claws, these tiny, near-blind pests feed on skin flakes, hairs, and blood.

flat body

strong, hooked legs

It's all Greek to me!
The scientific name for parasitic lice is *Phthiraptera*, which means "lice without wings" in Greek.

Lice advice
A louse is one of many lice.

HUMAN HEAD LOUSE
Pediculus humanis capitis

blood-filled gut

HEAD LOUSE ON YOUR HEAD

Humans aren't immune to these little bloodsuckers. A thick head of human hair is heaven for head lice, which attach their sticky eggs, called nits, to hairs. The body louse travels from person to person through the fibers of clothing. Only by washing with special shampoo and combing hair with a very fine comb can someone get rid of these annoying pests.

The color of a head louse depends on the color of a person's hair: a red head of hair = a reddish louse!

tiny eyes

slow moving

CRAB LOUSE
Phthirus pubis

3,2,1—
BLASTOFF!
A louse nymph swallows air to build up pressure inside its cramped egg. When the pressure is too great, the egg bursts and launches the newborn like a bottle rocket!

Thrips

Thrips climb up even the smoothest surfaces with sticky, inflatable pads on their feet. Fringed with tiny hairs, their slender wings allow them to glide with the wind. Sometimes called thunder bugs, thrips are known to take flight during thunderstorms.

COMMON THRIP
Thrips fuscipennis

hair-fringed wings

swollen, sticky pads on feet

It's all Greek to me!
The scientific name for thrips is *Thysanoptera*, which means "fringe wings" in Greek.

Thrips threat
Thrips are destructive pests of crops like pineapples, tomatoes, and beans.

27

True Bugs

All bugs are insects, but not all insects are bugs. Bugs all share the common characteristic of a strawlike snout called a rostrum. Tucked neatly under the head and thorax, the rostrum is a perfect tool for sipping liquid meals from plants and other animals.

thorax

hardened forewing

rostrum   **abdomen**

Basic Body Plan

Flip and sip!

TREEEHOPPER
Umbonia spinosa

Bush or bug?
Treehoppers camouflage themselves on plant stems and tree branches as thorns or other plant parts.

INDIAN CICADA
Angamiana aethera

SQUASH BUG
Diactor bilineatus

A real hard case
The shield bug gets its name from an extended part of its curved thorax. The colorful tough shield called a scutellum protects its transparent wings and soft abdomen.

Twenty-five thousand kinds of bugs inhabit a wide variety of places around the world, including water !

STRIPED SHIELD BUG
Graphosoma italicum

scutellum

GIANT WATER BUG
Lethocerus indica

hooked claw for grabbing prey

long, thin legs balance on water

POND SKATER
Gerris lacustris

breathing tube

Swimmers, Beware!
Giant water bugs adapted for life in tropical ponds and streams swim with paddle-like feet and hunt fish with massive clawed forearms. Skinny-legged pond skaters actually walk on the surface of the water in search of food. Breathing through long tubes on their rear ends, water scorpions hide in aquatic plants to surprise passing prey.

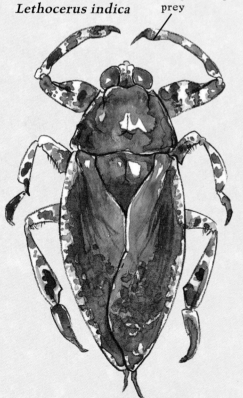

WATER SCORPION
Nepa cinera

28

Huge honkers
A lumpy-nosed lantern bug surprises attackers with a flash of its brightly colored wings and its intimidating snout!

Such a smelly fella
To deter a hungry hunter, a stinkbug releases a disgusting smell from its stink glands. Sometimes bright-colored patterns on its back advertise its smelly defense.

It's all Greek to me!
The scientific name for true bugs is *Heteroptera*, which in Greek means "half wing," for their half-hard forewings.

Killer Bug
An assassin bug stalks unsuspecting insects and injects them with a paralyzing saliva. The saliva helps the bug digest the insides of the doomed prey so it can suck out an insect shake! *Tasty, huh?*

What's that noise?
Cicadas are bug blabbermouths. Their mating calls actually originate from rigid membranes called tymbals in their abdomens. When these stiff tymbals buckle, they make a loud noise like the sound of a soda can being squeezed.
Hey, keep it down out there!

Don't let the bedbugs bite!
Bedbugs enjoy a comfortable bed at night, particularly one with a warm human body! The flat, wingless pests have caused many sleepless nights, since they feed upon human blood.

Baby bubbles
The nymphs of spittlebugs and froghoppers keep themselves from drying out by bubbling a protective foam around their squishy bodies.

Insect cattle
Aphids are troublesome crop pests that reproduce quickly and in great numbers. A hungry aphid slurps up liquid from fruits, vegetables, and flowers. Strangely enough, some ants protect the aphids, also called ant cows, and "milk" the aphids for sweet-tasting honeydew.

29

Beetles

Beetles are the insect world's biggest success story, with more than 300,000 different kinds known to exist! These adaptable survivalists developed thousands of different shapes, sizes, and lifestyles to fit into nearly every habitat on the planet. Beetles all possess a pair of hardened wing covers called elytra. Adapted from their front wings, the elytra serve as an armored shield for a beetle's delicate rear wings and vulnerable abdomen.

HARLEQUIN BEETLE
Acrocinus longimanus

backflips make a clicking noise

It's all Greek to me! The scientific name for beetles is *Coleoptera*, Greek for "sheath wings."

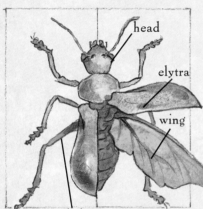

head

elytra

wing

speedy legs

Basic Body Plan

JEWEL SCARAB
Chrysina karschi

flashy exoskeleton may confuse attackers

COLOMBIAN CLICK BEETLE
Semiotus angulatus

Tiny to Titanic
Measuring $1/100$ of an inch, a tiny fungus beetle from North Africa can rest on the tip of a sharp pencil. The appropriately named Goliath beetle measures about six inches long and weighs nearly a quarter of a pound!

AFRICAN GOLIATH BEETLE
Goliathus goliatus

claws for climbing vines

Once a killer, always a killer
Speeding over the ground, the ferocious tiger beetle spends its life hunting for prey with scissorlike mandibles. Before it becomes an adult, the tiger beetle larva hides in an underground tunnel and snatches up any insect that passes overhead!

sharp jaws

BRAZILIAN LEAF BEETLE
Calispidea regalis

The ultimate pick-up artist

Named for their antlerlike mandibles, male stag beetles use their massive jaws in mating competitions over females. The frightening jaws of the male Chilean stag beetle are used like salad tongs to pick up and remove other male intruders from its home territory!

LADIES ONLY

Gas blast!

Bombardier beetles are nature's masters of chemical warfare. By mixing special chemicals inside its abdomen, this walking firebomb blasts unwary attackers with a blistering hot gas heated to nearly 100° Fahrenheit.

Shark beetles?

No pond is safe from the great diving beetle. With a pocket of air under its elytra, this bullet-shaped predator whips through the water after a meal of tadpoles and fish. Even its children are scary. The lethal larvae use tube-shaped jaws to suck up a liquid snack from captured victims. *Maybe I won't go swimming after all!*

A drink in the desert

Darkling beetles from the deserts of Africa collect dew from nightly mists on their upturned rear ends. Drops of condensed water roll down the grooves on the beetle's body and into its thirsty mouth! *I'll take bottled water instead, thank you!*

Flash twice if you're single

Fireflies or lightning bugs are actually beetles with glow-in-the-dark rumps. Special chemicals in the firefly's abdomen react and cause it to glow. When in search for a female of his kind, a male firefly flashes her a specific code with his shiny hiney.

Miniature morticians

Mating pairs of burying beetles search for dead animals to feed their children. Once a carcass is pulled into an underground burrow, the caring parents remain behind to clean the dead body and guard their defenseless larvae.

Violent violin

The flat-bodied violin beetle squeezes its form between bark and leaves in Indonesia. This fiddle-shaped hunter lurks under foliage and pops up to capture unsuspecting prey.

31

Weevils

Weevils are beetles equipped with an elongated snout called a rostrum. Biting mandibles at the tip of the rostrum enable the weevil to drill deep into plants and fruit. Some weevils cause severe damage to human crops. This is true of the boll weevil, which is infamous for destroying cotton plants.

MADAGASCAN WEEVIL
Eupholus linnei

elbowed antennae

elytra

rostrum

chewing mandibles

Basic Body Plan

Fleas

Unpopular bloodsucking pests, fleas live on the bodies of warm-blooded animals like dogs, chickens, and sometimes humans. The sides of their bodies are flattened so they can slide through dense fur and feathers. A flea's comblike spines latch on to the host animal when the ride gets rough.
Whoa, doggy!

FRONT VIEW OF A FLEA

blood-filled body

SIDE

HUMAN FLEA
Pulex iritans

comblike spires

piercing stylets

Dig in!
A hungry flea drives its spiked, sucking mouthparts, called stylets, into the host's skin to reach blood.

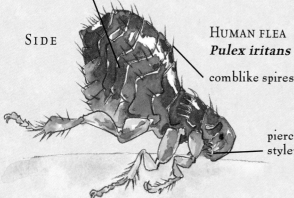

Baby bunnies and baby fleas
A flea's life cycle can be the same as that of their host animal. Chemicals in the blood of pregnant rabbits signal the rabbit flea to begin laying her own eggs.

Powerful jumping legs catapult these tiny, wingless parasites from host to host. If humans could jump as high and fast as a flea, they could hop over a skyscraper at about 180 miles an hour!

Rubber-band legs
Like a rubber band, the elastic material called resilin in the legs of a flea launches it into the air with a click, faster than the human eye can follow!

It's all Greek to me!
The scientific name for this diverse group of insects is *Siphonaptera*, meaning "wingless tube" in Greek, for their bloodsucking abilities and lack of wings.

Sand fleas really get under my skin!
Some fleas aren't satisfied with colonizing a host animal's fur. Jiggers or sand fleas burrow into the skin of animals and humans to lay their eggs.

Caddis Flies

Along the bottom of ponds and streams, the aquatic larva of the caddis fly drags its mobile home of shells, sticks, or seeds. Strung together with silken strands, the tubular case protects the soft body of the caterpillarlike larva. As the larva develops into a pupa, it crawls free and abandons the makeshift home.

It's all Greek to me!
The scientific name for caddis flies is *Trichoptera*, meaning "hair wing" in Greek, for the fuzzy wings of adult caddis flies.

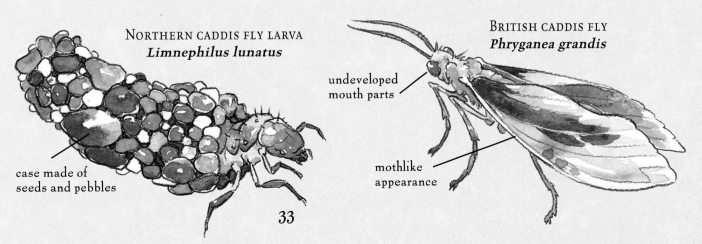

NORTHERN CADDIS FLY LARVA
Limnephilus lunatus

case made of seeds and pebbles

BRITISH CADDIS FLY
Phryganea grandis

undeveloped mouth parts

mothlike appearance

Ant Lions and Their Relatives

Ant lions, lacewings, alderflies, dobsonflies, and snakeflies all belong to a group of insects with carnivorous larvae and intricately veined wings.

Hole lot of trouble
Though adult ant lions look much like dragonflies, it is their lethal larvae that are famous. Ant lion larvae are frightening miniature monsters with long, tusklike mandibles. Sometimes called doodlebugs for the patterns they make in the sand, these crafty creatures dig cone-shaped holes for trapping unlucky ants and spiders.

It's all Greek to me!
The scientific name for this diverse group of insects is *Neuroptera*, meaning "nerve wing" in Greek, for their netlike wings.

clubbed antennae

two pairs of netlike wings

ANT LION ADULT
Tomatores citrinus

Lunch ho!
A snake fly on the prowl raises its head on its long neck like the periscope of a submarine to see over leaves and bark.

GREEN LACEWING
Chrysoperla rufilabris

large, shiny eyes

Tricky lacewings
Delicate nocturnal lacewings have special sensors on their iridescent wings for detecting bats. The skinny, dangling tail wings of a Mediterranean thread lacewing distract predators from its soft body.

Whooo's that?
Owl-flies are cousins of the ant lion, and have feathery bodies with large eyes like an owl.

OWLFLY OR
BUTTERFLY LION
Libelloides coccajus

Copycats
Mantispids or mantid flies look like a cross between a wasp and a praying mantis. Like a praying mantis, a mantid fly has powerful curved forelegs to snatch up a tasty insect meal.

veined wings

Time to get some waterproof boots!
Despite a gruesome appearance, the hooked mandibles of a male dobsonfly are just used to grasp the female during courtship, rather than to carve up prey. Unlike their parents, dobsonfly larvae are aggressive aquatic hunters and have earned the nickname "toe biters."

Scorpion Flies

Only male scorpion flies possess the upturned scorpion tails for which they are named. Biting mandibles at the end of their beaked snouts are helpful in scavenging dead insects, decaying plants, and pollen. While most scorpion flies hunt on the wing, the hanging scorpion fly dangles like a trapeze artist by its front legs to snatch up a fly-by insect snack.

It's all Greek to me!
The scientific name for scorpion flies and their relatives is *Mecoptera*, which means "long wings" in Greek.

HANGING FLY
Bittacus stigmaterus

dinner

Buggy burglars
Sticky spiderwebs are no trouble for the sneaky scorpion fly. Without alerting spiders, these web-walking thieves tiptoe across gooey webs and swipe trapped insects for themselves.

beak-shaped rostrum

curved, scorpionlike tail

MALE
SCORPION FLY
Panorpa nuptialis

A fly for the pretty lady
The male scorpion fly presents a dead insect or a glob of saliva to the female as a mating gift.
What, no ring?

35

Flies

Lots of insects are called flies, but true flies are aerial acrobats with only two wings and a pair of small paddles, called halteres, used for navigation.

Basic Body Plan

large range vision
haustellum
halteres
powerful wi[ng]

A liquid lunch for me

True flies are liquid feeders and have adapted special mouth parts, depending on their diet. Flower-feeders like the hover fly slurp up plant nectar with a long, strawlike snout, or proboscis. The bluebottle fly has a spongy mouth part called a haustellum for absorbing liquid food. Shaped like a doctor's needle, the sharp proboscis of a mosquito is perfect for piercing skin and sucking blood.

It's all Greek to me!

The scientific name for mosquitoes, flies, and midges is *Diptera*, meaning "two wings" in Greek.

Big-time buzzer

The wasplike mydas fly from South America is the largest fly in the world, and measures about 2 1/2 inches long!

Foot in mouth

The common housefly can actually taste with its feet! After landing on a suitable meal, he breaks down the solid food with a special digestive vomit and absorbs a liquid lunch with his spongy haustellum. **Didn't anyone teach him any table manners?**

BLUEBOTTLE FLY
Calliphoria vomitoria

FUNGUS GNAT
Macrocera stigma

stabbing proboscis
paralyzed victim

BLACK HORSEFLY
Tabanus atratus

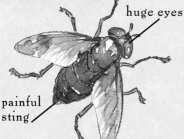

huge eyes
painful sting

Slurp 'n' burp

Bold robber flies attack dragonflies and grasshoppers often much bigger than themselves. These ferocious, bristled brutes stab their helpless victims with a sharpened proboscis and suck out the contents!

HOVER FLY
Syrphus ribesii

Wide-eyed flies

Bizarre stalk-eyed flies compete for territory by measuring their periscopic eye stalks against one another. A choosy, short-stalked female prefers the longer eye stalks of the winner for a mate.

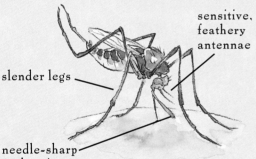

halteres

fragile legs break off if caught

CRANE FLY
Tipula lunata

Luminous larvae

The Glow Worm Caves of New Zealand are named for the twinkling larvae of fungus gnats that hang from the ceiling from silken webs. Unfortunate flying insects attracted to the glowing larvae and their webs are trapped and eaten for dinner!

Monster mosquito?

Spindly crane flies are often mistaken for giant mosquitoes. Unlike their bloodthirsty cousins, crane flies are nectar feeders and do not bite humans.

sensitive, feathery antennae

slender legs

needle-sharp proboscis

MALARIA MOSQUITO
Anopheles gambiae

His-and-her menus

The food of choice for lady mosquitoes is typically protein-rich blood, necessary for laying her eggs. Her feathery antennae can detect dinner targets from hundreds of feet away. Males, however, are vegetarians, and feed upon flower nectar.

Tired of flies

The bite of the African tsetse fly spreads sleeping sickness, a disease that causes extreme exhaustion and even death in humans.

A pest's pest

Culicoides anopheles, a tiny parasitic fly, steals a meal by sucking blood from the blood-filled mosquitoes.

TSETSE FLY
Glossina morsitans

Despite their pesky reputations, flies play a vital role in the environment. Pollinators like the hover fly help fertilize plants by carrying pollen from flower to flower. The squirming, legless larvae, or maggots, of blowflies and dung flies act as environmental recyclers by feeding on rotting flesh and animal waste. *Talk about stinky business!*

37

Butterflies and Moths

Butterflies, the beauty queens of the insect world, and their cousins, moths, are unique for the brilliant colors and elaborate patterns on their four large wings. These fluttering fliers are often compared to flowers and plants for which most have close relationships. The multicolored designs are made up of tiny scales that cover each wing.

Basic Body Plan

antennae

scales

coiled proboscis

It's all Greek to me!
The scientific name for moths and butterflies is *Lepidoptera*, Greek for "scale wings."

What's the difference?
At rest, butterflies fold their flashy wings up and over their backs, revealing often dull-colored undersides. Moths flatten their wings against their bodies and rest with the topside of their wings exposed. Even though butterflies are more visible, there are ten times as many moths in the world!

SPANISH MOON MOTH
Graellsia isabellae

Presto, change-o!
The metamorphosis of a butterfly is one of nature's greatest magic tricks. The wormy multilegged caterpillar emerges from its egg with only food on its mind. After gorging on a nonstop vegetarian buffet, the caterpillar takes a break to transform into a pupa, called a chrysalis. Inside the motionless chrysalis, the pupa's body metamorphoses, and soon a winged adult butterfly emerges.

BLUE MORPHO BUTTERFLY
Papilio rhetenor

shiny wings confuse predators

dull colors on underside of wings

Do Not Disturb!

Tough tots
Caterpillars take drastic means to defend themselves from predators. Flashy eyespots can startle unwary attackers while prickly spines make for a painful mouth-full!

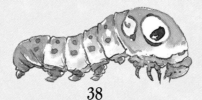

Big and small
One of the largest butterflies, the endangered Queen Alexandra's birdwing has a wingspan of nearly 11 inches and can only be found in select areas of Papua New Guinea. With a mere ⅜ -inch wingspan, the Western pygmy blue butterfly is tiny in comparison.

Monster moths
The atlas moth from Asia holds the world record for the biggest moth, though its South American cousin, the giant Agrippa moth, has the largest wingspan, measuring about 12 inches wide!

MONARCH
BUTTERFLY
Danaus plexippus

poisonous

PINK-SPOTTED
HAWKMOTH
Agrius cingulata

A long way to go for lunch!
Being nectar feeders, most butterflies and moths use a coiled, flexible proboscis like a drinking straw. With a proboscis nearly 13 inches long, Darwin's Hawkmoth of Madagascar dives deep into the bottom of orchids for a nectar snack.

Look out, Dracula!
Not all butterflies and moths sip nectar, however. The sharp, barbed proboscis of the dull-colored vampire moth of India pierces the skin of fruit and has even been known to feed upon the blood of mammals like deer and cattle.

Is there an echo in here?
Tiger moths warn predatory bats of their foul taste with distinct clicking sounds. A moth cousin, the banded woolly bear moth, tastes just fine, but copies the clicks of a tiger moth to keep from being eaten as well.

A moth to a flame
Night-flying moths use the moon to help them navigate through the darkness. It's no wonder they get confused and accidentally fly toward electric lights or right into campfires.

39

Wasps, Bees, and Ants

Under the guidance of a queen, bees, wasps, and ants cooperate in defending and caring for their ordered insect communities. Only the queen, mother to the entire colony, can lay eggs and is tended by her sterile female offspring, or workers. Most bees, wasps, and ants have four transparent wings and a thin waist. Although most ants are wingless workers, most male and queen ants do have wings for a short time during courtship.

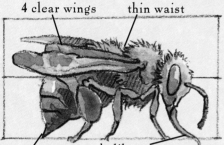

4 clear wings   thin waist

tubelike tongue

stinger, or ovipositor

Basic Body Plan

It's all Greek to me!
The scientific name for bees, wasps, and ants is *Hymenoptera*, which means "membrane wing" in Greek.

The stinger of a bee or wasp is actually a needlelike structure for laying eggs called an ovipositor. Equipped with venom, the hollow ovipositor can be used as a weapon to defend the nest from enemies.

COMMON WASP
Vespula vulgaris

powerful mandibles

DIGGER WASP
Chlorion cyaneum

She's a loner.
Not all wasps or bees live in large communities. The ichneumon wasp, like many other wasps, leads a solitary life. Hunting food for her young, the female drills her long ovipositor deep into wood in a search for elusive burrowing beetle larvae.

World's fattest bee

digs tunnels in wood

ASIAN CARPENTER BEE
Xylocopa laticeps

Wicked wasps
Pirate wasps lurk near bee-hives waiting to pounce on unsuspecting bees. Once a helpless bee is stung, this deadly marauder sucks out all her nectar and waits to stalk another victim.

Fuzzy, buzzy, bees
Buzzing loudly through the air, bumblebees carry pollen in special hairs on their hind legs called honey baskets. These large, hairy bees get their name from their irregular bumbling flight patterns.
Hey! Watch where you're going!

POLAR BUMBLEBEE
Bombus polaris

feathery wings

Teeny meany!
At a miniscule $1/200$ of an inch, the tiny myramid wasp may be the smallest insect on earth, but, by hunting crop pests, it helps farmers in a big way.

Talk about fresh food!
The world's largest wasp, the female tarantula hawk measures $2 3/4$ inches long and attacks full-grown tarantulas. After delivering a paralyzing sting, she lays eggs inside her eight-legged victim and drags it down a tunnel in the soil. The tarantula stays alive while the newborn wasp larvae feed on its living flesh.

Speaking the same language
Caution signs for humans are colored with yellow and black. Aggressive stingers like yellow jackets proudly display the same colors to warn any animal or person careless enough to bug them to back off!

A flower must have the pollen of another flower of the same kind to reproduce and grow seeds or fruit. Since plants can't move, bees do the job for them! During a day of pollen collection, a single honeybee can distribute the pollen of hundreds of flowers. Though they don't realize it, bees are just as important to the flowers as the flowers are to them!

Buzzing real estate
Inside a hollow log or man-made hive, honeybees sculpt a nest of stacked cells for newborn larvae and honey storage. The nest is built of wax that comes from a gland inside the bee's body.

Wasps construct a hanging nest from chewed-up wood fibers or mud. The nest's single opening is easily guarded and keeps enemies away from the vulnerable larvae inside.

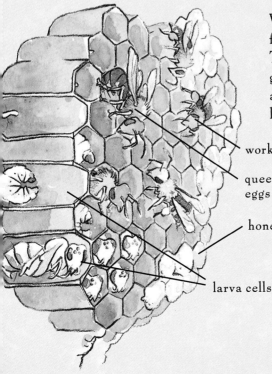

worker bee

queen laying eggs

honey cell

larva cells

worker wasp repairing nest

wasp queen laying eggs

larval cells

entrance

41

Mini muscle heads
One of the strongest insects in the world, the Amazonian leaf-cutting ant hauls cut-up leaves 50 times its own weight back to the nest. If you were as strong as these puny power lifters, you could easily carry a compact car home in your teeth!

Travelin' man
African driver ants never build a permanent nest and stay constantly on the move. Under the guard of massive soldier ants, the workers march over the forest floor, protecting their queen, carrying pupae, and attacking anything in their path.
Ten hut!

Lazy parents
Velvet ants are actually wingless female wasps. These crafty insect thieves break into wasp nests and lay their eggs on growing larvae. The velvet ant's larvae then devour the original residents and emerge as adults.

Child labor
Southeast Asian weaver ants use their wormlike larvae as sewing machines. A worker ant gently holds the larvae in her jaws as the wee web-weaver spins a silken thread between leaves or blades of grass, helping to build the colony's nest.

Just hangin' out
Filled with nectar, fat-bodied honey-pot ants from Australia and North America hang from the ceiling of the nest and act as living food storage containers for the entire colony.

AUSTRALIAN
BULLDOG ANT
Myrmecia gulosa

hooked mandibles

poisonous sting

RED IMPORTED FIRE ANT
Solenopsis invicta

Home Sweet Home
A colony of ants digs a complicated nest of underground tunnels to house workers, helpless larvae, and their egg-laying queen.

worker carrying food to nest

trash pile

queen laying eggs

ant larvae

fungus grown for food

Insects and Humans

Whether friends or foes, insects have always had an important relationship with humanity since the first human being stepped foot on planet Earth.

Six-legged symbols of the gods
Insects and their almost magical life cycles inspired myths and religious practices in ancient civilizations around the world.

Sacred scarabs
Scarabs are squat, shovel-faced beetles that lay their eggs inside balls of animal poop. Early Egyptians considered scarabs holy insects and even worshiped a scarab-headed sun god, Khepri.

dung ball

rolling scarab

Inspired by insects
Before becoming an adult, a cicada nymph must first shed its skin. Reborn into a new body, the molting cicada is an inspiring symbol of spiritual rebirth and reincarnation to Chinese Buddhists.

emerging cicada

old exoskeleton

Playing with clay
According to the myths of some South American Indians, the scarab Aksak sculpted the first man and woman from clay.

Flutters from heaven
The butterfly was a magical creature to the ancient Aztec and Maya of South America. They worshiped a ferocious goddess named Ixopalatl with butterfly wings and believed that butterflies carried the happy spirits of dead relatives.
Careful, that bug could be Uncle Sid!

WANTED
DISEASE CARRIER

Death, Disease, and Destruction

Despite their small size, the insect world has taken its toll on humanity.

Earth's most wanted: the mosquito

The title of Most Dangerous Animal on Earth goes to the mosquito, carrier of deadly disease, malaria. Every 12 seconds another human dies from malaria, caused by a bite from these lethal bloodsuckers.

Fatal fleas

More than just irritating little pests, fleas can be carriers of deadly disease. Millions of lives throughout human history were lost to the bubonic plague, known as the "Black Death." In unsanitary conditions, fleas can transmit the disease from black rats to unsuspecting humans.

WANTED
HAVE YOU SEEN THIS FLEA?

flea with plague   rat   dead rat

human   dead human

Loco locusts

Grasshoppers can be destructive crop pests. In warm dry climates, thousands of grasshoppers band together and become a swarm of locusts. Locusts have bright colors and voracious appetites, devouring all plants in their path. A swarm of African desert locusts can number up to 50 billion individuals and consumes 20,000 tons of vegetation in a day!

WANTED
FOR CROP DESTRUCTION

Homewreckers!

Termites are notorious for devouring wood in buildings and furniture. Bacteria and other microscopic animals inside the termite's gut help to digest the plant material.

WANTED
WORKS WITH THE TERMITE GANG

Pals, Pets, and Products

Not all insects are bad. In fact, many are used to control farm pests, make special products, or are even kept as pets!

SILKWORM MOTH AND SILKWORM

Bombyx mori

Milk them for silk

First produced in China about 3,500 years ago, silk is woven from the cocoon of the silkworm, a caterpillar of the silk moth. For its cocoon, a silkworm spins a silk thread nearly 3000 feet long! The cocoons are boiled in water, and the precious strands of silk are carefully unraveled.

Buzzing honey factory

Syrupy sweet honey is a mixture of flower nectar and bee saliva made inside the body of a honeybee. The nectar of nearly 23 million flowers goes into making just a pound of bee's honey!

The farmer's little helpers

Not just pretty little beetles, ladybugs are a gardener's best friend and an aphid's worst nightmare! Both adult ladybugs and their hungry larvae munch on juicy plant pests like aphids or greenflies. Mantids and wasps help farmers control crop pests without using dangerous chemical pesticides.

Broach or roach?

Native peoples of South America use the elytra of giant metallic buprestid beetles to make earrings and necklaces. In the Yucatan of Mexico, hump-backed zopherid beetles are decorated with glass beads and held on chains as living jewelry.

Bug dye

The red colored dye used for food and clothing is taken from the bodies of motionless budlike bugs called scale insects.

Can you find a leash that small?

Ancient Greeks kept caged crickets in their homes to enjoy their musical chirps. Children of Africa leash enormous Goliath beetles to sticks with string and watch the powerful fliers buzz around in circles.

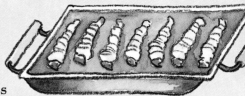

Insects as Food

Crunch and Munch

Packed with proteins, insects make the perfect snack for people all over the world.

Midges on the menu
Found in huge swarms over African lakes, tiny flies called water midges are collected and dried to make a breadlike food called *kungu*.

Dragonflies for dinner
Dragonfly nymphs are considered a delicacy in China. In Bali, people grill adult dragonflies over charcoal for a tasty treat!

Pop a hopper in your mouth
Grasshoppers and crickets are an important and delicious source of food for people all over the world. Fried in sizzling oil, grasshoppers make a crispy nutritious treat for people in Thailand. In Mexico, they are boiled, dried, and seasoned with onions, garlic, and chili powder.
Is there a recipe for cricket casserole?

Insect Experts: Entomologists

Entomology is a branch of science devoted entirely to insects. Scientists who study insects and their behavior are called entomologists. By understanding more about the complex lives of insects, entomologists can find ways to help people all over the world.

Into the unknown
Entomologists search the planet for undiscovered insects. From these findings, they hope to learn how insects affect the environment and also find useful new products or ingredients for human medicines.

Insect evidence

A bug can be a clue to a murder mystery! Insects found at a murder scene (or even inside the victim's body) by a forensic entomologist can help police investigators find a guilty killer.

Bug battles

Entomologists are soldiers in the war against disease and crop destruction. Their knowledge is vital for protecting crops from insect pests and stopping the spread of insect-transmitted disease without using dangerous pesticides.

Insect Conservation: Fading Fast

The world has become a crowded place. Today, humans share the planet with nearly 10 quintillion (10,000,000,000,000,000,000) insects! As the human population increases, the need for more homes, roads, farms, and natural resources becomes greater. Unfortunately, millions of insects are in danger of losing their natural homes. For example, the insect-rich rain forests of the world vanish at an alarming pace and it is estimated that some 60,000 different types of insect disappear with them each year. The permanent loss of just one kind of insect could upset the natural balance of an environment forever.

LONGHORN BEETLE

Bye-bye, big guy

The massive giant longhorn beetle is thought to be extinct due to increased logging and farming in Fiji. Other large insects like the Queen Alexandra's birdwing butterfly and the Hercules beetle are in serious danger as their rain forest homes disappear.

So, look before you step. Our world just wouldn't be the same without our six-legged friends in the soil, on the ground, and in the air!

The End